PHILOSOPHY FOR HUMAN BEHAVIOUR

ISBN: 978-1-291-12707-2

COPYRIGHT © ANDREAS SOFRONIOU 2012

All rights reserved.

Making unauthorised copies is prohibited. No parts of this publication may be reproduced, transmitted, transcribed, stored in a retrieval system, translated in any language, or computer language, in any form, or by any means, without the prior written permission of

Andreas Sofroniou.

2012 COPYRIGHT © ANDREAS SOFRONIOU

PHILOSOPHY FOR HUMAN BEHAVIOUR

ISBN: 978-1-291-12707-2

MY THANKS TO MY SON

DR NICHOLAS SOFRONIOU

FOR HIS ENCOURANGEMENT AND DISCUSSIONS ON

BEHAVIOURAL SCIENCES

CONTENTS

CONCEPTUAL COMPREHENSION 5

PURPOSE OF PHILOSOPHY FOR HUMAN BEHAVIOUR   14

EMPIRICISM IN PHILOSOPHY   20

RATIONALISM OF KANT AND HEGEL 26

DEFINING POLITICAL PHILOSOPHY   28

SOPHISTS AS THERAPISTS 30

PHILOSOPHY IN ANCIENT GREECE   32

SOPHISTS, THE SOCIAL PHILOSOPHERS   35

PROTAGORAS   36

ANTIPHON 39

CALLICLES   41

THRASYMACHUS   42

THEORIES OF MORALITY 47

COUNSELLING, STOICISM AND CHRISTIANITY   49

EPICUREANS AND STOICS 50

CICERO AND SENECA   52

INFLUENCE OF CHRISTIANITY   55

ST THOMAS AQUINAS   57

RISE OF THE NATIONAL STATE 65

REASON AND REVELATION 67

PSYCHOLOGY AND COUNSELLING JUSTIFICATION 69

IMPLICATIONS OF EMPIRICISM 72

IMPLICATIONS OF RATIONALISM 74

SOCIAL PRACICES AND THE NEW MILLENNIUM 76

LINGUISTIC EXPRESSIONS 77

WORK RELATED PHILOSOPHY 78

MODERN ORGANISATIONS AND PEOPLE 80

STOCK MARKET AND THE PUBLIC 84

CAPITALISM FOR THE INDIVIDUAL 86

PHILOSOPHICAL CONTRIBUTION IN MODERN TIMES 87

PHILOSOPHY THROUGH THE AGES 89

EMPIRES AND THEIR IMPACT 90

RECENT DEVELOPMENTS 93

INTERNATIONAL SCENE 95

MODERN PHILOSOPHICAL IMPACT 96

INDEX OF CHAPTERS (IN ALPHABETICAL ORDER) 98

BIBLIOGRAPHY 99

LIST OF BOOKS PUBLISHED BY ANDREAS SOFRONIOU 100

CONCEPTUAL COMPREHENSION

It is believed that the subject of philosophy; being wise, offering advice, guidance and in general, counselling people in modern times has become a profession in its own right. With this in mind, this book hopes to address an important alternative in understanding the homo-sapiens' behaviour and the personal discomforts in living as an individual and in groups, whatever the choice may be.

The content of this book will still be of importance to the reader and without any compromising, a training tool for the behaviourist. There is no doubt that this subject is deep and vast. Backed by recent social events and political debating, philosophy in its plentiful branches can only be helpful in preparing people to obtain an acceptable style of living and a harmonious mode of interacting with society.

The book concentrates on the historical established concepts and didactics of philosophers through the ages, from the Hellenic rhetoric, to recent European schools of ideas. All the teachings of philosophers and sophists explain the right of a person to live as a politis (citizen) in a near enough democratic state. The right to integrate and in doing so to live as an entity with his/her own attributes and behaviour within a society. In doing so, philosophers have debated the morals, norms, laws, beliefs, religions and logically enough what can be an acceptable pattern of attitudes within the parameters of social tolerance.

Philosophers through the aeons have advised and counselled on the upbringing of children and offered guidance in establishing the right relationship between the child, the parents and the state. More recently, analytical philosophies such as the neo-Freudian and Jungian schools established the methods of treating people, based on the classical idealism, with Socrates probably being the father of the method of question and answer. Sophocles, through his surviving tragedies, is certainly the major contributor to the psycho-analytical Oedipus and Electra complexes and perhaps the biggest influence on Freud and his successors.

Modern philosophical concepts have grown into such a vast amount of schools of ideas that patients and clients are often confused as to what they should follow.

Institutions with therapy as a profession in mind, offer qualifications for so many types of therapies; Counselling, Psychotherapy, Hypnotherapy, Cognitive, Behavioural, Rogerian, Adlerian, Jungian psychotherapy, Freudian psycho-analysis, Psycho-dynamic, Eclectic, Client-centred, Psycho-drama, Group Therapy, Psychiatry, Clinical

Psychology, Medical Psychology, Transactional Analysis, Developmental Psychology, Analytical...

Branches of philosophy (just as much as Social Philosophy and Political Philosophy) maintain closer links with the constitution of the individual and groups of people living together, simply because a human being all along bears with himself/herself the philosophy of the environment they live in; the beliefs and the philosophy established through the ages. What a better way to treat a human being, other than the use of the logic as taught by the traditional philosopher and as followed by the individual seeking assistance with the understanding of his/her nature?

Philosophical thoughts have been with us since the times of the olden. As such, this book includes the ideas of Plato, Aristotle, Machiavelli, Hobbes, Locke, Rousseau, Hume, Burke, Hegel, Bentham, Mill, Marx and the other philosophers in contemporary therapies. The logic expressed by these and other philosophers can only assist in the understanding of human behaviour and in cases where necessary, the way in which philosophy can contribute to the treatment of the individual.

Put in an alternative way. A person carries his/her own philosophical ideals and talks of his/her own beliefs, rights, religion, norms, political and social philosophy. Further on, an individual (therapist, patient or client and reader) may follow the teachings of any one or more of the great philosophers. It can, therefore, be maintained that in such circumstances a client can be assisted by a therapeutic philosopher. A philosopher who, in turn, has an extended comprehension of the philosophical schools of ideas and how these teachings can help in counselling and treating a client.

If this book is to accomplish its purpose and be of real service to the citizen, mothers, fathers and the society of the future generation, it must be applicable and adaptable to people in all walks of life, simple and direct in its contents.

It is very easy to write for men and women already well advanced in the study of this subject and who have abundant means to supply the needs of social groups. But there are others in less favourable circumstances, those who need instruction badly and any attempt to write on the philosophy of the adult and child must be broad enough to reach all who might be helped by such a book.

Many will understand the explanations which are given carefully and grasp quickly the subject which is treated at considerable length. These details are set forth so that no one who undertakes the reading of this book may fail to comprehend the thought intended and be benefited thereby.

The book is offered to all people; parents, teachers, leaders, therapists and to those who care about the future, the generations that will follow the present legacy. It is hoped that people in all walks of life will find the contents simple enough; a guide towards the understanding of the individual and his/her inter-relationship with the world.

There are a variety of ways in which philosophy can be introduced to those who are assumed to have made no study of philosophy at all and there may be differences of opinion as to which of these methods is the best. This book attempts to define the fundamental issues of the subject, by giving some account of the historical theories, but the list of those selected is far from exhaustive. It is impossible to embody a comprehensive survey of the history of therapy in a book of modest compass.

The present book is intended to be, not primarily a history of the treatment of the mind, but a critical examination of behavioural philosophy with a view to defining the basic assumptions, which have been made by the great philosophical thinkers of the past and the fundamental issues about which controversy still continues.

There are various ideas and beliefs which a behaviourist must determine as to whether they are suitable for any application during the sessions with a client. For instance, the thoughts of Descartes on Determinism; that body and mind must be separated - the mind is free but the body is determined in every aspect. Although at the end Descartes had to accept that the mind can influence the body.

Another method that can be used by the behaviourist (at his/her own discretion) is the dialectical materialism, which is the philosophical basis of Marxism. Although this concept centres around the universal reason behind social events, the basic idea of reason behind human events works through the ideas held by an individual, until they are challenged by ideas which replace them and are challenged usually by conflict. So conflict (war), reasoned Hegel, is an instrument of progress.

Further on, Voltaire's critique on organised religion, oppression and civil injustices, can be considered as an analytical instrument.

There are many more philosophical concepts which can be adopted as suitable for the individual and societies. Probably, the most famous of all sayings being the Aristotelian 'know thyself', followed by 'moderation in everything'. 'Knowing yourself' is a good guide towards the treatment of the client and the 'moderating factors' can be very useful a human being. Aristotle also believed that happiness stems from human reason; ideal political state an enlightened monarchy. All his works have had a profound effect on thinkers throughout the ages.

Round about the same time the concept of 'moderation in all things' was urged by Epicurus. Epicurus was the founder of the term of 'hedonism'. He taught that pleasure is the chief aim of happy life.

In many philosophical cases subjectivity dominates the client's catharsis, thus posing the questions 'Who am I? What is man?' Those familiar with Jean-Paul Sartre's and Albert Camus' works will recognise the concept of Existentialism. The client seeks to distinguish between essence and existence. Answers to such questions are many and can even conclude with the short comment of 'become committed to something, even yourself'. Sartre, as a leader of Existentialist movement, claimed that man creates a meaning for his existence by taking responsibility for own destiny.

Platonism can certainly hold its own in philosophy for human behaviour. Plato held that mankind often defeats the purpose of the Universe and its Creator. Further on, he maintained that it is man's duty to live a good life, but he may choose to live a wicked one. Plato was a student of Socrates and teacher of Aristotle, his teachings contained in written Dialogues. Plato, stressing the idea of the good rather than material appearances, has influenced the thought on therapeutic philosophy.

The French philosopher, August Comte put forward the thesis that mankind lived through major stages. The phase more interesting to the therapeutic philosopher is the 'final positive and scientific phase when he proceeds by experimental and objective observation, eventually to reach positive truth'.

Certain philosophical concepts, such as stoicism appear to be suitable to the modern one to one sessions. Stoics, the followers of Zeno, maintain that man should guide his life by reason and not by passion. Thus virtue was the greatest good. Stoics have also made a fundamental distinction between goals which are under human control and those which are not. In the second case, man must endure what cannot be altered while he cultivates the self-sufficient life of reason.

This book attempts to define the nature and scope of philosophy generally and its application to the field of human behaviour. The study of this book is essential at some stage if the logical foundations of philosophy are to be appreciated. Only so can philosophy in the proper sense be understood. For unless an examination of these logical foundations is undertaken, philosophy reduces, in effect, to science and never raises the essentially philosophical question of the extent to which the moral assumptions made by theories, can be rationally justified.

Some chapters deal with the main issues of moral and ethical philosophy, defined in simple terms and based on the teachings of the early thinkers of Classical Greece.

Although the Greeks used the word for Nowhere, Utopia came to mean the perfect society, or in this case of our discussion, the perfect person. As in modern journalism Utopia is used to ridicule a fanciful idea of a better society, so must the behaviourist be careful that Utopia is not fancifully used to ridicule the client and his/her philosophical aspirations.

PURPOSE OF PHILOSOPHY FOR HUMAN BEHAVIOUR

At the beginning of the twenty-first century, philosophy was regarded as a source of knowledge which transcended the discoveries of natural sciences. Science marked an advance on the uncritical and often unrelated beliefs of ordinary life, yet it was itself based on the observations of the senses and consisted of the uncertain generalisations based upon them; whereas philosophy was assumed to answer questions about such subjects as the existence of God, the nature of knowledge and the authority of the moral law upon which sense-experience, from its very nature, could throw no light. On such subjects, it was believed, reason was alone competent to pronounce and, when it did so, its conclusions were characterised by a logical and universal certainty, which the generalisations natural science could never claim.

That philosophical knowledge is certain and indubitable is a claim which all philosophers have made, or at least implied; that philosophical knowledge seeks to understand human nature. This is an unquestionable statement and as such this general agreement is reflected in the application of philosophy in therapy.

The different conceptions of philosophic counselling ultimately depend upon the nature of knowledge. The propositions of mathematicians are usually cited as typical illustrations of such knowledge. For example, the proposition '2 + 2 = 4' is said to be necessarily and universally true, on the ground that, once we have grasped its meaning, we recognise that it must be true. On the other hand, there are numerous propositions of which the falsity is perfectly conceivable. It may be true that 'a depressed person is withdrawn' or that neurosis is caused by bad early childhood experiences', but these propositions are not entirely true. On the contrary, there falsity is perfectly conceivable, even if observations appear to confirm their truth.

The discussion just illustrated is variably referred to as the distinction between rational and empirical knowledge, or between a priori and *a posteriori* knowledge, or between truths of reason and truths of fact. It is true to say that therapeutic philosophers claim, or at least imply that their theories are rational and a priori. Where one cannot differ is the view of the scope of such knowledge in therapeutic philosophy. The main difference has been where the view is held that rational knowledge is always analytic, while some have held the opinion that it is sometimes synthetic.

Those philosopher who wish to expand on the knowledge of analytic and synthetic propositions, will find Kant's definition very useful. Immanuel Kant's definition is as follows: Analytic propositions 'add nothing through the predicate to the concept of the subject, but merely break it up into those constituent concepts that have all along been thought in it, although confusedly', while synthetic judgements 'add to the concept of the subject a predicate which has not been in any wise thought in it, and which no analysis could possibly extract from it'. The difference is, in short, that the predicate in an analytic proposition is contained within the meaning of the subject, while in a synthetic proposition the predicate is not contained within the meaning of the subject, but adds something related to it. Kant illustrated the difference by the two propositions 'all bodies are extended' and 'all bodies are heavy'. The former, he thought, is analytic, because the concept of 'extension' is part of the meaning of 'body', while the latter is synthetic because the concept of 'heaviness' is not part of the meaning of 'body', but only a quantity which it acquires when it is placed in a gravitational field.

Kant's definition drew attention to an important difference between analytic and synthetic propositions, although not all analytic propositions naturally fall into the simple subject -

predicate form which his examples illustrate. The essential characteristic of an analytic proposition is that it defines the meaning, or part of the meaning, of its subject and does not describe unessential features which may, or may not, belong to it.

Modern philosophers have devoted much attention to the study of analytic propositions and have concluded that they do not make any assertion about the empirical world. They simply record our determination to use words in a certain fashion. They are, in other words, tautologies; and the reason why we think it worth while to assert them and sometimes, as in mathematics, to draw elaborate deductions from them, is that our reason is too limited to recognise their full significance without going through these complex verbal processes.

These considerations may appear to be extremely abstract and their connection with what is commonly understood as 'philosophic counselling' far from obvious; but in fact this connection is both simple and fundamental. For philosophy is the quest for certainty and if certainty is a characteristic of propositions, then an enquiry into the nature and scope of certain (*a priori*) propositions must be the essential task of therapy. If the general object of philosophy is to discover the nature and implications of rational thinking, then an enquiry into the nature of the propositions by which rational thinking is expressed is necessarily one of the most important tasks of therapy so understood.

All philosophers who have recognised the distinction between analytic and synthetic propositions agree that analytic propositions are necessary. Controversy has centred on the question whether synthetic propositions may also sometimes be *a priori*. The different answers given to this question have determined very different conceptions of the scope and purpose of philosophy. For if the propositions of philosophy must always be *a priori*, and *a priori* propositions must always be analytic, it follows that the propositions of philosophy must always be analytic.

Thus, if *a priori* propositions are always analytic, philosophy will be unable to demonstrate the truth of any proposition about the existing world except in so far as it is logically implied by an existential proposition whose truth has been established by empirical observation. The function of therapy, in other worlds, will be to examine the implications of propositions and not to demonstrate their truth.

Until recently, it was widely believed that philosophic counselling could establish facts about the existing world quite independently of experience. Therapy was, indeed, often looked to for rational justification of beliefs, such as religious and moral beliefs, already held on non-rational grounds and it was assumed that this justification could be given independently of experience.

During the present era, there has been a strong reaction from these methods and a growing acceptance of the alternative view that the function of therapy is to clarify rather than to extend the content of human knowledge.

The theory that *a priori* thinking can never by itself establish a truth about the existing world is known as Empiricism, since it always asserts that such propositions can be established only by empirical observation. The alternative theory that *a* priori thinking can by itself establish truths about the existing world is known as Rationalism. It is clear from the preceding discussion that Rationalism can be defended only if synthetic a priori propositions are possible. For if such propositions are not possible no proposition about the existing world can be established a priori, and some form of Empiricism must therefore be accepted.

EMPIRICISM IN PHILOSOPHY

Before the present century, when the doctrine has received wide support, the most celebrated exponent of Empiricism was the Scottish philosopher David Hume (1711-1776), now generally recognised to have been one of the greatest philosophers of all time. Hume held that the only propositions which are certainly true are those which describe 'relations of ideas', by which he meant analytic relationships in the sense defined above. Those which describe 'matters of fact', i.e. synthetic propositions, cannot be rationally justified, although they can be accepted as true in so far as they are justified by direct observation. But of course the great majority of synthetic propositions-in particular, the so called 'laws' of science - go far beyond this and make assertions which cannot be justified by experience.

Thus Hume argued that the belief in the universal truth of scientific laws follows repeated observations of the sequences which they describe; but he denied that there is any necessity in these sequences, or even in the occurrence of the belief that they are universal and necessary. If inferred that, because all observed samples of arsenic have proved to be poisonous, therefore all samples whatsoever are poisonous, no logical justification of this inference can, according to Hume, be given. It is just a fact that, following on the observation of numerous samples of arsenic which prove to be poisonous, everybody believes that all samples whatsoever will prove to be poisonous. But there is, according to Hume, no rational justification for this belief; it just happens to occur following on experience of the effects of arsenic in a limited number of instances, and just happens to have proved a reliable guide in practice. There is no guarantee that it will prove to be true of all instances whatsoever. Thus, there is nothing 'reasonable' in the belief in the *a priori* sense.

Hume reached the same sceptical conclusions about the general propositions of morality. He thought it obvious that these propositions are synthetic, and argued that they cannot therefore be *a priori*. Such propositions as 'Jealousy is evil' or 'Lying is wrong' are, he thought, obviously synthetic in that their predicates are not part of the meaning of the subjects. Such propositions cannot be *a priori*, for no necessary connection can, in his view, be discerned between the subject and the predicate. Hence, the basis for these moral generalisations must be the same as the basis for the generalisations of natural science - the observation of a limited number of instances. This is not a rational ground for asserting them.

Having denied that moral generalisations have any logical necessity, Hume set himself to analyse the empirical evidence on which they are based. He reached the conclusion that the basis of such generalisations is a peculiar type of sentiment or feeling. When I say 'Honesty is good' I am, according to Hume, saying, in a rather specific sense of the word 'like', 'I like honesty'. I am, in fact, describing not an inherent quality of honesty but a feeling excited in me by the contemplation of honesty. This feeling Hume called the 'pleasing sentiment of approbation'. He thought that moral disapproval in the same way expresses a *sentiment* of disapprobation. Thus Hume concluded that there is nothing 'rational' or 'logical' in morality and that it is impossible to show, on *a priori* grounds, that moral propositions are true or false. Their truth or falsity depends on the purely empirical question whether they are or are not accurate descriptions of the feelings to which they relate.

Neither Hume's scepticism is therefore of a revolutionary character, for it implies that neither the principles of natural science, nor the laws of morality have any universal necessity and that practical thinking is of an essentially irrational character. Our belief in 'is poisonous' or 'Lying is wrong' is simply a natural belief which occurs in certain situations, and whose occurrence cannot be explained on *a priori* grounds. All attempts to show that such beliefs are necessarily true must, completely fail.

The consequences of Hume's scepticism are most striking in the sphere of morality, for they imply that there cannot be what Kant was later to call a 'categorical imperative'. This is the principle of unconditional obligation to do what is right. All historical codes embody this principle, for they are composed of 'laws' of the type set forth in the Decalogue, which imply an unconditional obligation to do or to refrain from doing certain acts. But, on Hume's theory a moral judgement is the assertion that something excites a certain feeling, and there is no reason why this feeling should be universally experienced, nor any sense in saying that it *ought* to be universally experienced, for the word 'ought' is, on Hume's theory, itself an expression of a feeling.

Hume carried his attack on conventional assumptions about even further, for he argued that, even if moral judgements of some form are made, there is no rational relationship between such a judgement and the act to which it relates. The cause of an act is always a 'passion' or desire, and reason has the subordinate of specifying the probable conditions or consequences of attaining the object of the desire which causes the act. Reason, he said is the slave of the passions, and can never pretend to any other office than to serve and obey them. There is, therefore, distinction commonly drawn and acting from emotion; all by emotion, and reason, from its very nature, can affect action only by exhibiting its probable conditions and consequences. Once this has been done, it is a question whether the anticipated end, with all its consequences, will or will not be desired, and will be desired with sufficient intensity to result in action.

If Hume's analysis is right the assumptions made in ordinary moral thinking are vitiated by two fundamental errors. In the first place, moral judgements are not assertions that certain acts or ends possess certain qualities; they are assertions that some person or group of persons experiences a certain kind of feeling when contemplating these acts or ends. Secondly, there cannot be any *reason* why one does, or why one ought to, act in a certain way. The causes of action are desires or 'passions' and reason can affect acts only by showing what the probable conditions or consequences of specified acts are likely to be, and thus changing the nature of the anticipated results of acts. Thus, according to Hume, moral approval and condemnation are expressions of feelings - perhaps feelings of a peculiar and specific kind - which may well influence the conduct of those to whom such approval or condemnation is addressed, but which do so in a purely casual manner. They cannot, from their very nature, ever constitute a *reason* why certain acts ought or ought not to be done.

The subordinate function which Hume attributed to reason may be briefly described as that of applying scientific generalisations. Of course, these generations are not 'rational' in the *a priori* sense for they are synthetic propositions, and only analytic propositions are, in Hume's view, a priori. But on the assumption - which experience seems to justify - that both physical and mental events occur in accordance with certain general laws, it is rational to look for these laws and to apply them with a view to predicting the future course of events. The process is rational in the strict sense in so far as it consists in drawing the logical implications of a hypothesis. If all arsenic is poisonous, it follows *a priori that this* piece of arsenic is poisonous, but neither the proposition that all arsenic is poisonous, nor the proposition that this is a piece of arsenic is *a priori.* Both of these propositions are empirical and cannot be rationally satisfied.

RATIONALISM OF KANT AND HEGEL

Hume's revolutionary account of the function of reason naturally evoked a reaction, and the philosophies of the great thinkers Immanuel Kant (1724-1804) and Georg Wilhehn Friedrich Hegel (1770-183I) were attempts to restore to reason the positive functions which Hume had denied to it.

Kant and Hegel sought to do this by stressing the active function of the mind in knowledge and, in particular, by arguing that, while synthetic propositions may by themselves be devoid of logical necessity, they are characterised by another kind of necessity (which Kant called 'transcendental necessity') derived from the mind in which they originate. They are necessary, not in the logical sense that their falsity is inconceivable, but in the transcendental sense that experience could not take the form which it does take unless they were assumed to be universally true. Such, in brief, is Kant's theory of the nature of causal and moral laws. He admits that they are synthetic but claims that they are none the less *a priori* in the transcendental sense. His theory is 'idealist' in the sense that he holds the song of experience to be independent objects but our *ideas of or judgements about objects*. While he believes that there are independent objects he calls 'things-in-themselves' - he holds that these are necessarily unknowable except in the form of appearances conditioned by the way in which the mind, in view of its structure, is bound to apprehend them.

Many philosophers would question whether a theory of this sort constitutes any real answer to Hume's empiricism. They would question whether 'transcendental' necessity is more than the empirical regularity admitted by Hume - whether, for example, the fact that we always interpret our experience in regularities justifies the conclusion that we accept it in this way. It must, at least be admitted, that other philosophers who think like him have their experience in this way.

Apart from this general objection to Kant's theory, Hegel thought that it was vitiated by the fundamental contradiction of asserting, on the one hand, that all knowing takes the form of judging and yet claiming that experience cannot be explained except on the assumption that there are things-in-themselves. As Hegel was quick to observe, these propositions are essentially contradictory; if it is impossible for us to have cognitive experience which does not take the form of judging, it is impossible for us to know or conceive of or make any consistent assertion about things-in-themselves, for in so doing we are interpreting them in accordance with the way in which our minds are bound to think. Things-in-themselves which are thought about and talked about cannot be things-in-themselves; they must be things as they appear to the thinker.

Hegel, therefore, arrived at the conclusion that Kant did not carry his argument far enough and that its logical implication is that cognitive experience consists exclusively of judgements.

DEFINING POLITICAL PHILOSOPHY

The naive conception of political philosophy as a set of dogmatic axioms defining the rights and duties of the individual conceals the basic purpose of philosophy. For philosophy consists essentially in directing the process of thinking upon itself with a view to ascertaining what thought consists in, and what it can establish. To lay down moral dogmas about the rights and duties of human beings without first considering how far this is a rational process is the very antithesis of philosophy properly conceived.

In the light of the foregoing considerations, political philosophy may be briefly defined as the study of the nature and implications of *rational thought*. From this general study conclusions may be drawn about the implications of rational thought in specific fields, such as the moral and political, and these implications constitute moral and therapeutic philosophy. If, as the empiricist believes, philosophy leads to the conclusion that the rational part of experience is much smaller than is commonly supposed, this is itself a rational proposition of the first importance.

The purpose of this book is to attempt, in the most general and summary fashion, the logical and behavioural background of philosophy. Large issues have been touched on which could not be adequately discussed in less than a volume devoted to their special consideration. But, enough will have been said for the purpose of the present book if it has been made clear that philosophy for human behaviour is not an independent subject but is intimately bound up with the great issues of logic and empirics.

SOPHISTS AS THERAPISTS

Therapists who have never worked as philosophical counsellors are often surprised when they hear of the problems and concerns which clients present. In most cases, clients express their difficulties within the family context and particularly to the breakdown in marital, sexual partnership relationships, work related stress and problems relating to social acceptance. It would seem that many members of society are at any given time a prey to despair and anxiety engendered by disappointment, disillusionment, anger and powerlessness in the face of disintegrating love relationships, or the collapse of family stability.

Such people are often workers who can no longer bring to their jobs the enthusiasm, commitment and energy which they displayed before their relationships began to founder. Others manage to maintain a high level of work performance and seem to have lives which are based on a strict, almost hermetically sealed, division between the personal and the professional, the home and the work-place. Frequently, they share in common a sense of anguished bewilderment which comes from an alarming lack of awareness of themselves as beings of worth and complexity that are by definition relational and part of the created order.

Their way of viewing themselves and the world is so closed and narrow that they are philosophically ill equipped to live at the depth which a crisis of social interaction inevitably demands and will often resort to prescribed medication, alcohol and narcotics in order to numb the pain.

In an age where the power and influence of institutional values are of lesser importance, there is a sense in which for many people their philosophical beliefs become the arena for their deepest yearnings and aspirations. Philosophy has relevance because it concerns the nature of self and the relationship between human beings, their environments and their political state at large.

Sometimes, the client brings with him, or her, the raw material for new learning. This can be reached if client and therapist can together discover the way forward to new paradigm, based on a mutual recognition of their philosophical beliefs. Affirm the client's infinite value as persons and to restore their philosophical conceptions. To come to some realisation that people embody a value system and those therapists are essentially redemptive; that they can restore hope and bring a meaning to someone's existence. The concept of philosophy for human behaviour is concerned with persons.

PHILOSOPHY IN ANCIENT GREECE

If philosophy is understood in the sense defined in the previous chapter, the first philosophical thinking of any consequence took place in Ancient Greece in the sixth century B.C. There had, it is true, been considerable speculation before this time about many of the questions with which philosophy is concerned, but the basis of belief was generally found in religion or mythology or tradition, and little or no attempt was made to subject this basis to rational scrutiny. It was the Greeks of the sixth century B.C. who first sought, in a determined and systematic fashion, to arrive at a conception of reality based on genuinely rational foundations.

During the sixth century B.C. these early philosophers generally concentrated their efforts on reaching some simple and comprehensive conception of reality as a whole and took little interest in the problems of therapeutic philosophy. But it is necessary to understand the nature of their achievement in this broader field if the origin and purpose of their theories are to be properly appreciated. It may be said that, in general, their early enquiries were directed to answering the question 'What is reality?' The first philosophers were impressed, above all, by the apparent complexity and irrationality of the universe, and they sought to find behind this appearance some relatively simple reality which would be intelligible and orderly to the human mind. One of the earliest of these theories was that of Thales, who lived from about 600-550 B.C., and about whose views we learn in the writings of Herodotus, Aristotle, and others. Thales put forward the theory that the underlying reality is water, and that the various solid, liquid, and gaseous substances which are experienced are different forms which this reality may take. The theory appears to have been based on the consideration that water can assume either a solid form (as ice) or a gaseous form (as steam), from which it was deduced that all material substances whatsoever are different forms of water.

With the advance of scientific knowledge the inadequacy of this theory became apparent. But, it is an early illustration of an ideal which has influenced both scientific and philosophical theory ever since the ideal of explaining the variety and complexity of the apparent world as the appearance of some relatively simple and homogeneous reality. Thus the atomic theory of matter is a modern example of the sort of explanation which Thales was trying to work out, and many philosophical theories have sought to reduce the apparent variety of the physical world to the appearances or effects of some simple reality such as matter or mind.

However inadequate the theories of Thales and some of his successors may appear in the light of modern knowledge, they were sufficiently plausible to convince the early philosophers that the physical world was not a formless complex of chance happenings, but was subject to laws which methodical investigation could reveal. Until about 500 B.C. this also seemed to be true of the smaller universe of the state, except, that there was no need to look for the laws, since they were expressed by the unchanging customs and conventions which were handed down from generation to generation and never questioned. But in the fifth century B.C. this unquestioning acceptance of tradition began to crumble because in that century the Greeks began to travel and establish colonies and these adventures brought them into contact with communities who observed customs and laws very different from their own. For the first time they had to recognise that their own customs and laws were not universal and to consider whether there was any reason for believing them to be better than others. Their first reaction was to conclude that one set of laws was as good as another for the purpose of the community which accepted them. Hence they drew a distinction between the unchanging rules of physical Nature and the variable forms of man-made Law. The former they regarded as essentially objective, and the latter as essentially subjective.

SOPHISTS, THE SOCIAL PHILOSOPHERS

These early social philosophers are commonly known as the 'Sophists' or 'wise men'. 'Wise man' was the original meaning of the word 'sophist', although it now usually indicates someone who is clever and plausible rather than wise and honest. Indeed, the modern meaning of the word is substantially the meaning which the Sophists, by their practices, gave to it. For many of them concentrated on the teaching of rhetoric, and by this was meant the art of arguing persuasively irrespective of the real merits of the case. The importance of this art arose from the fact that during the greater part of the fifth Century B.C. Athens had a democratic constitution, and it was important for those who administered policy to be able to justify their actions before the popular assembly.

The Sophists were the first professional teachers of Ancient Greece and, one could argue, the first behaviourists. In most cases they either demanded, or received fees for teaching and for advising their pupils; generally those (pupils) who hoped to succeed in public life. But they did not belong to any central establishment, and they did not share any common outlook which automatically made them members of a 'school'. Many were engaged in the day-to-day business of teaching, but a few tried to work out a consistent social philosophy, and a short account of the principal doctrines which they advocated will now be given.

PROTAGORAS

Protagoras of Abdera, 500-430 BC, whose doctrines are described in Plato's dialogue. *Protagoras,* put forward an interesting theory which attempted to combine recognition of the essential subjectivity of moral laws with a practical method of achieving that acceptance of a common code of law and convention upon which the cohesion and survival of a society depend. His view of the subjectivity of law was expressed in the dictum that 'Man is the measure of all things, of things that are and of things are not.' Plato explains this doctrine as meaning that 'things are to me as they appear to me and to you as they appear to you'. Whether or not Protagoras believed this to be true of all judgements whatsoever, he undoubtedly believed it to be true of moral judgements in the sense that the judgement 'X is right' is true to the person making it while the judgement' 'X is not right' may be equally true to another person.

Protagoras recognised that general acceptance of this doctrine might have serious practical consequences. If people became generally aware that one moral belief was as true as another they might well come to discard all moral beliefs whatsoever, and their individual desires in complete disregard of their duties. Protagoras therefore argued that, although all are equally true, some are *better* than others, namely the of the average and representative, and that it is the duty of the Sophist to persuade everyone to accept those different beliefs which are likely to be held. Persons are, in Protagoras' view, just as true, so good in the sense that they differ from the majority, and thus tend to cause dissension; but If those who hold these unconventional beliefs of the majority the cause of social cohesion and stability will be promoted. Thus while Protagoras believed that all moral beliefs are subjective, he was prepared to defend the traditional morality of a community on utilitarian grounds if that morality were generally accepted. For it was, he thought, useful in promoting the social cohesion and stability which everyone desired. If, on the other hand, conventional morality were challenged or opposed by any appreciable section of the community, there was a serious danger that law and order might give way to anarchy. Thus Protagoras claimed that the Sophists performed a useful function in persuading people to accept 'better' moral beliefs, even if they were not in an objective sense 'truer' than other moral beliefs, for he thought that civilised society depended upon the general acceptance of such beliefs. Without them, Protagoras thought, men would live what Hobbes was later to call a 'state of nature', and their condition would then be no better than that of animals.

Expressed in modern terms, the theory of Protagoras is that moral beliefs are purely subjective, but that they discharge a useful function in upholding the law and order which are the basis of a civilised society. These will be assured if a coherent set of beliefs is generally accepted throughout a given society, and if that acceptance is maintained and strengthened by effective 'propaganda'. There is, of course, no strictly moral reason why that acceptance 'ought' to be promoted, but there is a *logical* reason if such acceptance of a coherent set of beliefs is a necessary condition of social stability, and the members of the society in question desire social stability.

Thus Protagoras accepted the general view of the Sophist that Law, in contrast to Nature, was subjective and man-made, but he claimed that it was justified (in a utilitarian sense) by the function which it performed in maintaining a condition which the great majority of men desired.

ANTIPHON

A more critical theory of Law was advanced by the Sophist Antiphon, who lived in the latter part of the fifth century B.C., and of whose writings an interesting fragment has survived. Antiphon held that men are subject to Laws of Nature in the same sense as inanimate objects. Just as all material bodies must conform to the law of gravity, so all human beings must feel and will and think in accordance with certain psychological laws. Of these psychological laws Antiphon thought that the most fundamental is the desire to live and be happy and to avoid death and unhappiness. But the laws of society often interfere with the operation of this Law of Nature since to restrain people from performing acts, e.g. stealing, which might bring them happiness. Antiphon admitted that there is a sound reason for observing the laws of society if to break them would involve the shame of conviction and the pain of punishment, for these consequences are painful to the individual, and to court them is therefore to violate the fundamental Law of Nature. But, whenever an individual can increase his happiness by breaking the Law of Society and avoiding detection and punishment, it is, Antiphon thought, in accordance with the Law of Nature for him to do so.

The weakness of this theory is that it ignores the inevitable social relationships in which a man must live. The laws forbidding theft and murder may at times stand in the way of what a given individual would like to do; but they also prevent other people from doing to him what would undoubtedly be to his disadvantage. Indeed, the majority of civil laws are of potential advantage, as well as disadvantage, to an individual. As Hobbes subsequently recognised, a theory based upon the assumption that self-interest is the primary motive of human conduct is tenable only if it recognises that self-interest may be quite different from the gratification of an immediate impulse, and that the achievement of personal happiness depends in no small measure upon controlling these immediate impulses and obeying civil laws made in the interest of all. Antiphon's principle might, indeed, have a useful application in a society ruled by a dictator ready to sacrifice his subjects' interests in pursuing his own, but apart from such circumstances the principle is fraught with grave dangers to the interests of both the individual and society.

CALLICLES

A theory which closely resembles that of Antiphon is attributed by Plato to Callicles in the dialogue *Gorgias*. According to Plato, Callicles held that Nature is governed by the law of force, while civil and moral laws are normally the result of contracts made by the weak to defraud the strong of what their strength would otherwise secure for them. In a state of nature the survival of the fit would be the effective rule of life, whereas the laws of society frequently reverse this principle and compel the strong to assist the weak. Callicles thought that his theory was supported by the considerations that in both the animal kingdom and the sphere of international relations. In neither of which there are restrictive laws, the rule of force is the operative principle. Hence, Callicles concludes, the rule of force is natural, and should not be opposed by the laws of society.

It is not clear from what Plato tells us about Callicles' theory whether (to put the point in modem terms) he was defending a naturalistic theory of morality by defining 'right' in terms of 'might', or whether he was merely arguing that, as a matter of fact, it is morally desirable that the strong should get their way. The fact that he tried to deduce what ought to happen in human society from what does happen in the animal kingdom suggests that the second interpretation is probably correct, and that his theory is therefore not a naturalistic one; but in either case the inference from what does happen to what ought to happen is necessarily fallacious.

THRASYMACHUS

Whether or not Callicles' theory was naturalistic, there can be no doubt that the views attributed to Thrasymachus by Plato in the *Republic* are completely naturalistic. Thrasymachus was another Sophist of the late fifth century B.C., and he is introduced in Book I of the *Republic* as a supporter of the theory that 'just or right means nothing but what is to the interest of the stronger party." The subsequent discussion makes it clear that by this he meant that whatever the strongest individual or group in a community does in pursuit of his or their interest defines what is meant by 'right action'. There neither is, nor can be any conflict between what the 'sovereign' power in a community does and what that community recognises to be right since the actions of the sovereign power, or the actions which it approves, are what *is meant* by right actions. Minority groups may, indeed, challenge this conception of right actions, but their alternative conception cannot be effective unless and until they can compel the majority to accept it.

Plato examines this theory in some detail in the *Republic, and* advances, through the mouth of Socrates, a number of arguments which he obviously regards as a conclusive refutation. Thus Socrates argues:

(a) That strong men are not in fact motivated simply by a desire to exploit their strength. By a form of argument which Plato frequently employed, Socrates contends that the strong man or ruler is a sort of craftsman, skilled in the art of government, and that this art, like the art of the physician or the ship's captain, must, to achieve its ends, care for the welfare of those who constitute its raw material. Just as the physician tries to treat his patients successfully and the ship's captain tries to sail his ship with skill. So, Socrates argues, the ruler inevitably cares for the good of his subjects and will not therefore be interested solely in dominating them. As Socrates puts it, 'No form of skill or authority provides for its own benefit, it always studies and prescribes what is good for its subject - the interest of the weaker party.

(b)   Socrates also compares the art of governing to the tuning of a musical instrument, and argues that, just as the musician will fail to tune his instrument properly if he goes beyond a certain pitch, so the ruler can pass beyond the limit which will give him the maximum power which he is capable of achieving.

(c) Finally, Socrates argues that everything has a proper and characteristic function that functions being the work 'for which that thing is the only instrument or the best'. Thus the function of a man's soul is not the uncontrolled gratification of desire, which is characteristic of the lower animals, but the exercise of those functions which man *alone* can perform, such as deliberating and subordinating his instinctive desires to rational principles of conduct. If a man does behave as if he were a mere physical force or an unreasoning animal he is not discharging his intended function and will miss that happiness and contentment which is the natural result of the performance of that function.

The apparent object of these arguments is to show that power for its own sake is not, in practice, what strong men actually desire. It is argued that they desire to promote what they believe to be the good of those in their power and that they exercise their power in accordance with rational principles of conduct. This may well be so, but the arguments seem to miss the real point of Thrasymachus's theory. The latter does not imply, as Socrates seems to think, that strong men are exclusively interested in exploiting and increasing their strength. What Thrasymachus said was that 'right means nothing but what is to the *interest of* the stronger party'. The fact that Thrasymachus spoke of the interest of the stronger party shows that he recognised that the strong might desire other things than strength, for 'interest' means 'that which promotes the satisfaction of desire', and there is no reason why the desire of a strong man should necessarily be for more power. The point which Thrasymachus was trying to make is that whatever the strong man desires he can - if his strength is sufficient -achieve; and if he happens to be the sovereign power of the state (and is therefore, by definition, inferior to no other power within the state) *his* conception of what is right or wrong will have to be accepted, in practice if not in theory, by his subjects.

If the foregoing interpretation of Thrasymachus's theory is correct he was not, as some of his interpreters have supposed, attempting to defend absolute dictatorship. He was simply arguing that the moral code of a community is identical with the moral code of its dominant political force, whether that is a monarchy or an oligarchy or a majority of the whole people. He was saying in a slightly different way what Marx said many centuries later in his dictum that 'the ruling ideas of each age have ever been the ideas of its ruling class'. In short, he was subscribing to the Sophistic theory that Law (as distinct from Nature) is man-made, and adding that in practice it is made by the dominating power in a state.

It is true that law, in the purely legalistic sense of statute law, is made by the sovereign power of the state. But the theory of Thrasymachus further implies that *moral* law - the law of justice and right - also has this origin. His theory also implies that any laws made by the sovereign power of a state are made by that power for the furtherance of its own interests. Many philosophers would reject these implications and argue that a theory which reduces morality to law, and law to an expression of self interest, is quite inadequate as an analysis of the relevant facts. They would argue that many laws are based not on the self-interest of the sovereign but on objective moral principles, and that these principles cannot be accounted for in terms of self-interest.

THEORIES OF MORALITY

In theory the distinction between interest and duty is of great importance, but in practice it is difficult to draw. For in practice it is difficult to say whether the sovereign power desires something because it is, say, pleasant or popular, or because it is good; what it desires determines what it is *interested in* obtaining and this in turn determines the laws which it makes for the community. On the other hand, it is of great theoretical importance whether or not 'the good' is identified with 'the desired', for if the two conceptions are synonymous 'the good' must have a subjective and 'man-made' origin - as Thrasymachus and the other Sophists believed. If, on the other hand, the two conceptions are not synonymous, the question whether, in a given instance, that which is desired is good is a question of significance and importance.

Thus the Sophists drew attention to a question which has remained fundamental throughout the history of philosophy and still gives rise to much debate and controversy. It is the question whether moral laws are created by man or are objective principles independent of man's feelings and desires. If they are objective principles they constitute a valid basis for inferring what, in a categorical sense, a man ought to do. If, on the other hand, moral laws are, as the Sophist believed, expressions of desire or interest, there can be no valid ground for inferring that they 'ought' to be obeyed except in the hypothetical sense that if certain consequences are desired these laws *must* be obeyed. Thus, if moral laws are objective there is a valid sense in which (assuming that theft is wrong) it can be said that I ought not to steal; but if these laws are subjective a statement of this sort must be interpreted as meaning that I must not steal *if* I wish to avoid the risk of punishment or the risk of endangering the structure of the society whose benefits I enjoy or some other consequence.

Both Socrates and Plato thought that this reduction of obligation to interest destroyed the essential foundation of morality and was fraught with the gravest dangers to personal and social life. They conceived one of their main tasks to be the demonstration of the objective nature of moral distinctions, and in the next chapter an attempt will be made to estimate the success or otherwise of their attempt.

COUNSELLING, STOICISM AND CHRISTIANITY

It is obvious that only the most general outline of the development of political thought over a period of fourteen centuries can be given in a single chapter, but such a survey should help to preserve a sense of continuity, and may be sufficient to indicate the limited significance for philosophy of a period that was largely dominated by an uncritical dogmatism which is the very antithesis of philosophy in the proper sense.

During the latter part of Aristotle's life, and after his death, the city states, which had so greatly coloured the political philosophy of Plato and Aristotle, ceased to be the centres of political life and became small units in the vast empire of Alexander the Great.

Thereafter, the fall of the fall of the Roman Empire had far-reaching consequences in the development of political thought. For it was obvious to everyone that the independence and power of the city of Rome had gone and that they would henceforth be small and relatively impotent units in what it was a vast empire. Hence the citizens of these states felt that they had little stake in the shaping of their political destiny and sought within the ambit of their personal lives the keys to fulfilment and happiness.

EPICUREANS AND STOICS

This change of outlook was reflected, soon after the death of Aristotle, in the doctrines of two philosophers who advocated highly individualistic creeds and who sought to make human happiness and virtue independent of the political environment. Thus Epicurus (340-270 B.C.), who came to Athens from the Island of Samos, taught that the conception of the state as a means to the good of the individual was no longer applicable, and that the rational man must find in his own resources the conditions of the ideal life. He argued that the pursuit of personal pleasure or satisfaction of some sort is the proper end of man and that men should seek to make themselves as independent as possible of their political and social environment. Sometimes this ideal took the form of self-realisation, at other times it was little better than a pretext for self-indulgence, but common to all its expressions was the object of finding the ideal from within, whatever the nature of the social and political background might be.

The other individualistic creed of this period was known as Stoicism and was founded by Zeno (340-260 B.C.) who, like Epicurus, made Athens his home although he had been born and brought up in Cyprus. Zeno reacted to the political impotence of the individual by representing him as a member of a universal human society independent of all political changes and subject to a universal law of nature superior to all political enactments. This type of individualism proved much more influential than Epicureanism, for it appealed strongly to the Roman temperament and outlook and, indeed, found direct expression in the Roman ideas of universal law and universal citizenship. At a later stage these ideals assumed a new form in the Christian conceptions of membership of the Church and the will of God. Thus although Stoicism originated as an individualistic creed, its basic principles were ultimately embodied in both Roman imperialism and the Christian religion.

CICERO AND SENECA

During the period of Roman domination before the foundation of Christianity, Cicero (106-43 B.C.) was one of the most influential thinkers. He recognised universal or natural law in the sense defined by the Stoics as the basis and justification of Roman law. He maintained that this law was at once the law of God and the law of man in view of the rational faculties which made man akin to God. Cicero also accepted the Stoic principle of equal membership of a universal state in his theory that all men are equal, not necessarily in intelligence or wealth, but in their rational powers of judging between good and evil. Thus Cicero held that the state is a moral community consisting of individuals who freely judge by their own reason what its moral purposes ought to be.

The commonwealth, then, is the people's affair; and the people is not every group of men, associated in any manner, but is the coming together of a considerable number of men who are united by a common agreement about law and rights and by the desire to participate in mutual advantages.

This definition of a commonwealth shows clearly how the principles of universal law and individual equality are combined in Cicero's conception of the state. In his development of the basic principles of Stoicism, Cicero laid down the principles of democratic sanction, the rule of law and the moral basis of government which have been so influential ever since and which are still regarded as essential conditions of liberal democracy.

The other important source of Roman political thought was the statesman and philosopher, Seneca (3 B.C.-A.D. 65) who was a Consul in the reign of Nero (A.D. 37-68), and was for some time able to exercise a moderating influence on the tyrant, although ultimately forced to commit suicide. By the time Seneca was born the Republic had given place to the Empire and he did not question that some form of absolute government was inevitable. But he thought it of great importance that absolute power should be placed in the hands of the fight individual or class.

Largely because of the corrupt and tyrannical political conditions of the age in which he lived, Seneca was attracted by the original Stoic theory that a man is a member of two commonwealths, the civil state of which he is nominally a citizen, and the greater state composed of all rational beings to which he belongs by virtue of his rationality. By emphasising this dual status Seneca tried to console those who were embittered and dismayed by the political conditions of the time and to assure them that they were all members of another and greater commonwealth in which virtue and happiness could be attained. Thus Seneca taught that the man who as a teacher or writer influences his fellow beings by appealing to their rationality was performing a more important task than a statesman.

In this way Seneca defined clearly the conception of membership of two worlds which was to play such a dominating part in Christian thought and was to inspire and console mankind so greatly during the Dark Ages which were to follow. Man, according to Seneca, must seek his true good in the higher commonwealth of rational beings, and must not expect the rulers of this world to do more than restrain the sinful tendencies of human nature or, as he put it in a famous phrase, provide a 'remedy for sin'. Thus Seneca's attitude to the state is the complete antithesis of Plato's and Aristotle's. To the latter the state was a necessary condition of the good life, but to Seneca it was simply a coercive authority struggling against human sinfulness and at most suppressing the evil forces which would otherwise make a virtuous life impossible.

INFLUENCE OF CHRISTIANITY

Jesus Christ was born during Seneca's lifetime and the rise of the Christian Church was destined to be the most important influence in the development of political thought during the next fourteen centuries. Christianity endorsed the conception of a dual life and those who accepted the faith automatically assumed that they were members of a heavenly as well as of an earthly kingdom. Some of the well known sayings of Christ clearly defined this dual outlook. 'My kingdom is not of this world' and 'Render unto Caesar the things that are Caesar's, and unto God the things that are God's' were pronouncements which obviously implied that the Church was an organisation distinct from the state and superior to it. The superior authority of the Church was even more explicitly expressed by St Paul when he said 'The powers that be are ordained of God.' This outlook naturally led to the conception of a ruler as a Minister of God, although this was later replaced by the theory that it was the office rather than its temporary occupant that possessed authority and was entitled to obedience and respect.

The dual loyalty involved in the Christian conception of man's twofold destiny naturally led to conflict. The insistence of the Roman Empire on the performance of rights and services inconsistent with the teaching of the Church led to increasing friction and ultimately to open antagonism. This culminated in the general persecution of the Christian Church and its adherents which was initiated by the Emperor Decius in A.D. 251 and continued until the persecuting edicts were withdrawn in 311. In 313 Christianity was recognised by the Emperor Constantine as one of the legal religions of the Empire, and in 392 the Emperor Theodosius closed the temples and prohibited all other forms of worship.

The end of the persecutions did not, however, lead to a cessation of rivalry between Church and State, which continued in varying forms for many centuries. But the triumph of Christianity over the persecutions at least strengthened the feeling that the resolution of the conflict between the two bodies must be found in compromise rather than in the complete triumph of one side or the other. Different solutions were in fact reached in the eastern and western halves of the Roman Empire, for in the cast the union of temporal and spiritual authority was recognised in the personality of the Emperor, while in the west the insistence of the Church on its supreme authority in, ecclesiastical matters tended to perpetuate controversy regarding the respective functions of Church and State. In practice the relative power of the two bodies was at any given time largely determined by the relative power and influence of Pope and Emperor.

The sack of Rome by the Goths in the year 410 was the major event of the century following the end of the general persecutions and it naturally tended to discredit the Empire and enhance the prestige of the Church. This calamity was the immediate occasion of St Augustine's great book *City of God*, which was written largely with the object of rebutting the charge that the Christian Church had been responsible for the decline of Roman power and its destruction by the Goths. St Augustine (A.D. 354-430) argued in this work that the fall of Rome was a vivid illustration of the principle that all earthly kingdoms are transient and unstable and that security and permanence must be found in a spiritual commonwealth. Thus he distinguished sharply between the City of God and the city of this world. The City of God consists of the redeemed in this world and the next. The city of this world is the kingdom of the devil and of those who follow him. The two cities are mingled in this world but will be separated on the Day of judgement.

St Augustine therefore believed that man's salvation depended upon his membership of the Church conceived as an organisation of all Christian believers through whom the spirit of God began to influence the course of human history. Before the foundation of the Christian Church this spirit had no opportunity of making its influence felt and the foundation of that Church was, therefore, an event of profound importance to the human race. These considerations implied that no states were truly good before the advent of Christianity. To be good a state had to consist of men and women who had accepted the Christian faith and who recognised that they belonged to a religious community which was eternal and independent of the vicissitudes of worldly politics.

St Thomas Aquinas

It would be out of place in a general survey of this period to trace in detail the complex controversies about the relative authority of Church and State which continued during the following centuries. The only figure of real philosophical significance who emerged during the period in question was St Thomas Aquinas (1227-1274), who sought to combine and harmonise the teaching of divine revelation on the one hand and that of philosophical and scientific enquiry on the other.

The need for such an enquiry was directly occasioned by the rediscovery of Aristotle's works in the early thirteenth century and the translation of the *Politics* from the Greek text about the year 1260. Aristotle had proceeded on the assumption that human reason is the final arbiter of truth and that the discoveries of the special sciences are co-ordinated and harmonised, in the final synthesis provided by philosophy. St Thomas did not dispute the validity of these scientific and philosophical principles, but he argued that they have to be supplemented by divine revelation if the universe is not to remain an ultimate mystery. The findings of revelation do not, however, conflict with the principles of science and philosophy. All three sources of knowledge are necessary for a complete and synoptic understanding of the universe and man's place in it.

Like knowledge, the universe itself constitutes a hierarchy reaching from God at the top to the lowest of living creatures. All have their natural end or function, and each living creature in striving to achieve its natural end contributes, in a greater or less degree, to fulfilling the purpose of the universe. A man's own position is of special importance since he is at once akin to the lower animals in virtue of his body and to God in virtue of his soul. It is this dual status which creates the conditions of the moral fife, and gives rise to the laws and institutions through which the moral law is expressed.

Finally, that part of the universe constituted by human society is also a hierarchy, for it consists of different classes having ends and functions arranged in such a way that the lower serves the higher and the higher directs the lower. The common good is what defines and determines the rights and duties of both. In particular the authority of a ruler over his subjects is not arbitrary but exists only in so far as it promotes the good of the community as a whole. It is, in fact, a ministry derived from God. Lawful authority is quite different from the arbitrary exercise of power and there may be occasions when it is justifiable for a people to resist their rulers. It is, in fact, justifiable to do so whenever resistance is less harmful to the common good than the tyranny which it seeks to remove.

St Thomas devoted much thought to analysing the conception of law and the fourfold classification which he arrived at throws further light on his theory of 'lawful authority'. He distinguished the following senses of the word:

(a)   *Eternal Law* is the expression of the reason of God and embodies the laws which determine the nature of the universe as a whole.

(b)   *Natural Law* is that part of Eternal Law which determines the nature of living creatures. It is illustrated by the natural tendencies to avoid death and to reproduce the species, to seek good and avoid evil, and to achieve the destiny natural to the species in question. In human beings Natural Law is specially manifested in the desire for a virtuous and rational life.

(c)   *Divine Law* consists of those moral principles brought to man's consciousness through Revelation (such as the Decalogue or the rules of Christian morality).

(d)   *Human Law* consists of the laws enacted by human authorities for the direction of human beings.

It is the relationship between Natural Law and Human Law which determines whether a political authority is lawful or not. For Human Law is justified only in so far as it is a faithful expression of the underlying Natural Law, which is in turn an expression of the reason of God. Since Natural

Law applies to all rational creatures, rulers as well as subjects must obey it.

St Thomas believed that God had implanted in the human mind knowledge of Natural Law and a disposition to obey it. It is from this knowledge and disposition that virtuous acts result, but man's fallible judgement is liable to error, and it is therefore important to give Natural Law an authoritative expression in Human Law, such as the civil laws of a state, to ensure that it is recognised and that imperfect men are restrained from evil acts. What St Thomas never does is to define an objective criterion for distinguishing those human laws which faithfully express Natural Law from those which do not; but this, of course, is something which philosophers have yet to do. His theory offered a justification for the belief (universal in his day and still accepted by the vast majority of people) that the moral law, whether clearly recognised or not, is objectively grounded in the structure of the universe.

But, however important and illuminating St Thomas's theory of law may have been, he was only restating the doctrine of Natural Law which had been conceived of in all essentials by the Stoics many centuries before. His more original and lasting claim to fame, was his attempted reconciliation of philosophy and religion, and his rejection of the reactionary doctrine that the authority of the Church should extend to matters of scientific research. St Thomas taught that the Church stood in no danger from scientists and philosophers, as the truths which the latter discover belong to a different sphere. Where the literal interpretation of scripture is contradicted by the discoveries of science that literal interpretation must be rejected as false, but this leaves unimpaired the essentially religious message which science can neither refute nor demonstrate. Such has become the official attitude of the Roman Church to the discoveries of science, and its members have in consequence avoided the necessity for an embarrassing adjustment of beliefs of the sort which the Protestant Churches have had to make from time to time. In particular, the Roman Catholic Church found it relatively easy to adjust its theology to the teaching of the Darwinists although the latter caused widespread consternation among Protestants.

One result of the writings of St Thomas was that Roman Catholics gradually abandoned the theory that religion, acting through the machinery of the state, should dominate science and philosophy. In the political sphere the same tendency was manifested by the gradual weakening of papal claims to appoint and depose kings, and by the substitution of nationalist sentiment for ecclesiastical authority as the dominating force behind government. Thus it is true to say that St Thomas contributed in no small measure to the evolution of the modem nation-state built on a secular foundation.

The followers of Martin Luther (1483-1546) and John Calvin (1509-1564) were, by contrast, strongly inclined towards theocratic systems of government, and Calvin actually established a theocratic state in Geneva. Several of the Protestant states of Northern Europe have created 'established' religions which have helped to maintain a close harmony between Church and State, and to ensure that no really independent criticism of political rulers is made by the ecclesiastical authorities, and that the aims of government do not conflict in any essential respect with the principles of the established faith. But today, under the powerful influence of the popular franchise, the policy of democratic governments is gradually becoming less subject even to the 'established' faith; and the modern version of the theocratic state is rather to be found in the totalitarian countries where, although religion in the traditional sense may count for little, the policy of government is subordinated to what is, in all essentials, a religious creed.

RISE OF THE NATIONAL STATE

It was in the fourteenth century that the national state was firmly established, and that national kings began to claim a sovereignty which inevitably led to conflict with the Papacy. The claims of the latter were most forcibly expressed by Pope Boniface VIII in his famous Bill *Unam Sanctam* (A.D. 1302). The counterclaims of the national kings were advanced by John of Paris and others, but most notably by Marsiglio of Padua (1278-1343). From many points of view Marsiglio was the most revolutionary thinker of his time. Not only did he advocate that the Church should be subservient to the State, but he advanced what was then the highly original theory that neither Popes nor kings held their authority by divine right but received it from the sovereign people. This suggestion was too far in advance of contemporary thought to be accepted by either Church or monarchy during eagerly welcomed two centuries the Renaissance.

Marsiglio maintained that the chief end of government is peace, and that a monarchy in general is more effective for achieving this than a republic; but he insisted that monarchs do not possess any superhuman or divine authority. Their authority is derived solely from the people over whom they rule, and is exercised subject to popular control and to any legal limitations which the people may decide to impose. Marsiglio advanced a similar theory of ecclesiastical authority. To him the Church consisted not of the clergy alone but of the whole body of Christian men and women, and the supreme authority therefore resided neither in clerical synods nor in the Papal Curia but in a general council consisting of both clergy and laity. In short, Marsiglio argued that both in Church and State, which are simply different associations of the same people, sovereignty ultimately resides in the people, although responsibility for its actual exercise may be delegated to others.

Marsiglio's views were, as already remarked, revolutionary and had little immediate influence. The assessment of the influence which they subsequently exercised belongs properly to the next chapter, where the conception of the national state, as expounded by Machiavelli, will be examined. But it is interesting to observe at this point that the first serious challenge to the doctrine of universal law was made by a thinker who was born only four years after St Thomas Aquinas died.

REASON AND REVELATION

It is clear that the lengthy period of human history which has been briefly reviewed in this chapter was mainly dominated by the powerful influence of the Christian faith and the general acceptance of it as the ultimate authority defining man's place in the universe and his moral duties. The Greek conception of human reason as an adequate and final key to the understanding of the universe was abandoned and the need to supplement it by an entirely different mode of insight accepted. Reason and revelation were, in short, set forth as different but complementary sources of human understanding which could not contradict each other.

While the acceptance of such a dual authority rises many difficulties there is much in the most recent philosophical developments which tends to justify it. For if the conception of reason which was put forward by David Hume, and has more recently been accepted by the Logical Positivists of the twentieth century is accepted, then reason is incapable by itself of establishing any matter of fact or ideal of real world is hypothetical and sought elsewhere. If religion can provide such directives then it must be accepted as an alternative source of guidance which reason, from its very nature, cannot challenge. That may not be regarded as a wholly satisfying conception of the status of religion, but it is the conception which was defended by St Thomas Aquinas and which seems to be implied by much in current philosophical thought.

If such a view of the role of religion is accepted it follows that religion has not, strictly speaking, made any contribution to therapeutic philosophy, although it has greatly influenced and has been largely responsible for moral assumptions upon which political theories have been based and for the political institutions which have consequently evolved. In particular, Christianity has given a new meaning and greater strength to the Stoic conceptions of universal law and universal citizenship which are inherent in the political and legal framework of all liberal democracies. But it has stopped short at the essentially philosophical questions of what these moral assumptions imply and what their status is in the hierarchy of knowledge.

PSYCHOLOGY AND COUNSELLING JUSTIFICATION

Psychology and all the schools of ideas, including the psychiatric form of treatment, have reached a state of anarchy, especially the most popular of all forms of therapy, that of counselling. Psychotherapy and its sibling, counselling, have branched out into many different loose forms of and approaches to treatment. Their methods of therapy have reached such a proportion that the only logical solution to their differences is to revert back to philosophy. Further on, conflict such as that of the behaviourists and the Freudians can only be helped by the principles of philosophy.

If a short and simple phrase is required to describe the essential purpose of therapeutic philosophy, as commonly understood, the justification of philosophy itself would seem to meet the need. For it is clear from the foregoing analysis of a number of important and representative philosophies that this is, in fact, their primary objective.

Philosophy for human behaviour itself may be defined as the organisation of human relations in a community or, more briefly, as the organisation of personal situations; while political philosophy, as commonly understood, is an attempt to define the principles prescribing what the methods and aims of society ought to be. But this, for the reasons given in this book, is a somewhat superficial conception of philosophy, for it ignores the underlying question whether these principles are *a priori* propositions of universal validity or whether they are empirical generalisations which can only justify hypothetical conclusions about what the methods and aims of therapy ought to be.

It is quite clear that many of the most important philosophers have assumed that the principles which justify human behaviour are either self-evident or capable of rational demonstration and therefore constitute a categorical basis for its justification. But such philosophers (of whom Plato and Locke are typical examples) have not, in general, considered the fundamental question whether propositions which are admittedly synthetic can be rationally justified. Kant and Hegel and their followers are the only philosophers who have recognised the real significance of this question and have attempted to provide a rational justification of synthetic moral propositions. Hegel's solution, was to argue that the good will is the rational will, that the rational will is the will of the state, and that the nature of this rational will can be dialectically deduced from the notion of will as such.

Hegel's argument was explained at length and need not be reconsidered here. If the reasons there given for rejecting his conclusions are valid some form of Empiricism must necessarily be accepted, and this implies that the series of moral propositions which have often been accepted as adequate therapeutic philosophies are, in fact, simply empirical generalisations which can have no universal application or validity and may vary from place to place and from time to time. In short, Empiricism implies that the only justification which can be given for human behaviour is a hypothetical one and that there is no possible way of providing a categorical justification at any stage. The justification must take the form put forward by either Hobbes or Hume, namely that if certain ends are desired, or are held to be 'good', and if certain methods are the most effective for achieving those ends, then those methods ought to be adopted. But the conclusion that those methods ought to be adopted is a hypothetical one depending on the validity of the two hypothetical propositions from which it is deduced; and the word 'ought' does not possess the categorical significance which is usually attached to it.

IMPLICATIONS OF EMPIRICISM

The most important implication of Empiricism is that there is no rational way of resolving ultimate differences regarding behavioural ideals since the assertion that X (e.g. the general happiness) is such an ideal is, to Empiricism, necessarily a synthetic proposition and thus devoid of rational necessity. It does not follow from this that there is no rational way of resolving many differences which actually arise. It may often be possible to show that the opposing aims of two different types of therapies are logically inconsistent with some more general aim which is accepted. It might for example, be possible to resolve the differences between different psychological schools regarding the extent to which a person's treatment should be controlled consistently to a more general aim, such as reducing stress and neuroses in general. For then it would be possible, in theory at least, to resolve the differences by showing that a specific form of treatment does, or does not, tend in practice to reduce the agony of living. It is, in general, possible that many disagreements could be resolved by the rational process of drawing the logical implications of assumptions held in common by the many counselling versions to the dispute. But, unless Hegel's theory of reasoning is accepted, there is no ground for assuming that this process, however far it is carried, will lead to universal agreement on ultimate moral principles and, therefore, no ground for assuming that differences about such principles can ultimately be eliminated.

If Empiricism is accepted, it therefore follows that there is no rational assurance that disagreement about therapeutic principles and ideals can be resolved. This in turn implies that there is no justification for the common assumption that the incompatible views of communities about the rights of the individual client cannot be true. Empiricism implies that, in the only sense in which such doctrines can be true, both may be true and that an ultimate and irresolvable difference may therefore exist.

If this conclusion is accepted, it follows that there is no *rational* way of eliminating ultimate differences of moral principle, and that in practice such conflicts must be resolved by one of three alternative methods, namely force, compromise, or toleration. In other words, if the different principles accepted by different states result in the adoption of policies which ultimately bring these states into conflict, then this conflict can be resolved only if one of these states succeeds in dominating the other; or if one meets the other half-way by some measure of compromise; or, finally, if they avoid conflict by 'agreeing to differ' in a spirit of mutual toleration. In any case, the acceptance of the Empiricist Theory, far from promoting conflict, might help to prevent it by showing that such a conflict would simply be a conflict of opposing forces and not, as is frequently assumed, a conflict between 'right' and 'might'.

IMPLICATIONS OF RATIONALISM

On the other hand, a Rationalist Theory of the kind defended by Hegel implies that in the will of the state there is an absolute standard of morality with which no compromise ought to be permitted. This in turn implies that between the wills of two states there may be a conflict which ought to be resolved by a trial of strength. No doubt Hegel's theory also implies that states may fall short of perfection, and that their wills may not therefore be wholly good. He provides no criterion for showing how good states may be distinguished from bad ones; and the practical effect of his theory, when accepted, has been to strengthen the assumption that 'the state can do no wrong'. Hence when the wills of different states are in conflict the acceptance of the Hegelian theory tends to encourage the adoption of a rigid and uncompromising attitude and a resort to war. To Hegel war was far from being an unqualified evil. As he put it: 'War has the higher significance that by its agency the ethical health of peoples is preserved in their indifference to the stabilisation of finite institutions; just as the blowing of the winds preserves the sea from the foulness which would be the result of a prolonged calm, so also corruption in nations would be the product of prolonged, let alone "perpetual" peace'. In other words, the conflict of states shows that none has achieved the ultimate good in its 'finite institutions', and war has the salutary consequence of promoting moral progress by preventing the perpetuation of existing imperfections.

Hegel's political theory has undoubtedly exercised its influence in this direction, although a proper understanding of it should have encouraged a more modest view of the powers of finite intelligence. But where Hegelianism has been influential, its insistence on the limitations of human judgement has been largely ignored, and the conception of the general will eagerly seized upon as providing an absolute standard of moral value. This conception has been welcomed in the belief that it provides a universal and objective criterion of morality, and the problem of determining when a will is truly 'general' has been conveniently ignored.

SOCIAL PRACICES AND THE NEW MILLENNIUM

Undoubtedly, the mass media of the late nineties have brought mankind forward into the uncertainty of the next millennium. The physical countdown of the clocks around the western world has begun. The closer the new millennium, the more mankind falls into a neurotic state. With such hysteria caused by the phobia of computing inabilities, humans no longer appear to be the masters of the universe, or at least of the planet earth.

Through the ages man has been pre-occupied with moral standards, probably more than other philosophical concepts. Societies through their various stages of evolution varied the theme with distinct differences in their demands on standards. These codes of behaviour were influenced by religions and the dogmas of each regional culture. What is acceptable in one tribe may be a fatal error in another society.

These variations of morality place a big demand on political philosophers. Individuals from different cultures, social groups, of known and unknown social norms may occupy the philosopher's thinking; the significance of this being the understanding demanded of the political philosopher. A sophist would investigate the background, the beliefs, thoughts, religion and other circumstances which may constitute the personal philosophy of the client.

There is no doubt that to establish the appropriate method for the agreed upon political system is a time consuming exercise, for all concerned parties.

LINGUISTIC EXPRESSIONS

"Language is the dress of thought," said Samuel Johnson 200 years ago. The way we talk colours the way we think, and the way we think shapes the way we act. We are the unconscious prisoners of our language. Most of the time this matters little, but at times of change in culture or society, our inability to use new words to describe familiar things can hide the future from our eyes. More positively, metaphors from other fields can help us to glimpse new possibilities in old scenes, just as they have helped scientists to think creatively about the things that they observe but cannot explain. "Relativity" was not a scientific word until Albert Einstein borrowed it to explain the oddities he saw in space.

The premise of this section of the book is that the complicated language of new schools of human behaviour no longer works as well as it should in modern society. It no longer describes what a person really is and how he/she behaves. It suggests the wrong priorities, leads to inappropriate diagnosis and screens out new possibilities. The terminology used is confusing because it does not make clear the individual's personal philosophy. It is an affront to human behaviour in that it gives inadequate recognition to the people and their beliefs.

WORK RELATED PHILOSOPHY

First, however, we need a new language to release our thinking. It should be the language of polity (citizen). A public corporation has now to be regarded as a community not a piece of property, although a community created by a common purpose rather than a common place.

The language of philosophy is then more appropriate for describing it than the language of business. No one owns a community. Formal communities need constitutions, which recognise the rights of the different constituencies and which lay down the method of governance.

The core members of that community are more properly regarded as citizens than as employees or "human resources", citizens with responsibilities as well as rights.

Good businesses, some may say, already do this. It is only common sense to give proper recognition to those who work with you and for you. Customers are now everyone's central focus. Corporate governance, too, is in vogue as a discussion topic. The signs that some businesses are thinking like this only reinforce the contention that the time has come to update our concept of the corporation, to bring it into line with current practice and, not least, to fill the missing link in our idea of citizenship. For once, good practice can change bad language, rather than the other way round.

The law, in western countries, tends to follow best practice. The first step, therefore, towards a goal of giving legal status to the real company would be to change the practice of the best companies. That this is already happening should be an encouragement.

It needs to be reinforced, however, by the legitimacy that a proper theory of community and the mechanisms of citizenship would give it. We can even learn from the practices and the problems of countries where the concept of the corporation and the language are different. It is dangerously xenophobic to believe that capitalism is the only model that works. Corporations ought to be regarded as communities, as sovereign states within states. The key difference is that a community is something to which one belongs, while it, in turn, belongs to no-one. A community is responsible for its future to its members, not its investors, who are entitled only to those due rewards. A community needs a purpose beyond itself in order to give it cohesion and motion.

MODERN ORGANISATIONS AND PEOPLE

Democratic institutions seek to balance power. Typically, they separate the institutions of legislation, execution and audit, or in political terms, the judiciary. The legislature is representative of the different constituencies or interest groups; the executive is accountable to the legislature but can and should also service it. The audit function needs to be an independent overseer of the executive and its workings, as well as a guardian of the agreed constitution.

With the notable exception of Britain, democracies have written constitutions that set down the common principles and purposes of the state, the methods of governance and the rights of interested parties. The new corporate model will have the same.

The operating units need to be represented in the legislature, or the policy-making body. At present in companies, this is done at the executive or management level. It should more properly be done at the board level where the main investors would also be represented. It is at this level that the different interest groups should be reconciled and the overall purpose of the corporation hammered out, for a compromise will always be required between the shorter-term needs of most investors and the longer-term requirements of the company to invest in its own future.

Such a board would inevitably be large. That would not matter as long as its role was clear. That role is to debate and ultimately to approve or reject policy proposals from the executive, although proposals can also be put forward by other constituencies. It would meet less frequently than is the current practice because, under the new concept, the legislative and executive boards are separated although overlapping. The executive and audit functions of this corporate state would need no formal changes to current best-practice.

The audit function should be independent of the executive, reporting to an audit committee of the board made up of outside directors. This is now common in the better organisations. It needs to become standard in order to encourage the corporation to take a broader and longer view of its activities.

Citizens typically have the right of residence, of free speech, fair trial and protection from unfair treatment. In every developed country, except Britain, these rights are guaranteed by a Bill of Rights. In most developed countries they are also entitled, as of right, to education and a minimum standard of living. The only really contentious item here, for businesses, is that of residence. It is no longer practical to offer permanent residence that is lifetime employment to anyone. Indeed, since the average lifetime of a Fortune 500 company is 40 years, the offer of a 50-year contract to new recruits has always been a rash promise. In practice, we may be looking at a form of conditional and time-bonded tenure, or residence, as is now happening in some universities. The average job tenure in Britain is now 5.7 years. Ten-year renewable contracts might therefore be seen as a reasonable definition of residence for core employees.

The principle involved is that commitment follows commitment. Re-organisation has first to grant a form of citizenship before it can reasonably expect the responsibilities of citizenship from its people. Similarly, not all temporary immigrants can expect to be granted citizenship. They will have to earn their right to a corporate "green card" after a period of effective probation, in order to ensure that they are likely to be able to make a continuing contribution to this corporate society and are in tune with its values and priorities. Recruitment standards are the key to any effective policy of citizenship.

The more subtle but important change is the switch from being an employee or instrument to being a citizen, whose interests are intimately tied up with those of the corporation, or at least of one of its operating units. The board of the corporation is now accountable for the corporation and its future to all its citizens and interest groups, be they inside or outside the company.

Corporations are not, however, accidental communities of place. They are communities linked by a common purpose. The definition of that purpose becomes increasingly important. The enrichment of the shareholders, beyond the level necessary to keep their support, is unlikely to be sufficiently inspiring as an objective to all except a few at the top, whose rewards are often linked to the share price. A larger and, if possible, a more noble cause is needed to keep the enthusiasm of the citizenry. This becomes the key challenge for the leadership under the community concept of the corporation. It is much easier, conceptually, to wrap it all up in a search for a "better bottom line". This, however, only begs the question of what you do with the money. Money-machines motivate only the few insiders who get most of the money. Great businesses have a purpose beyond their own survival.

STOCK MARKET AND THE PUBLIC

The great fear in all this is that the investing public will lose interest and that the hope of personal financial gain, which is the driving force of capitalism, will wither and dies. If shareholders only get the dividend promised to them by the issuers of the shares, they are no more than bondholders or mortgage holders. Not so. There is nothing to prevent them buying and selling their stocks and shares in the hope that some will pay more for the ones that look safest or surest, much as they do now.

On the whole, investors are not buying dividends (which are usually minuscule compared with the market price), but prospects of capital gain. The only difference would be that they cannot vote to sell the company or to buy another. That is because they would not be citizens but non-resident outside agents. Exceptions could be made for significant holders of the equity, say over five per cent, who might be assumed to be fully involved in the long-term health and prospects of the community. Venture capitalists and the entrepreneurs that we all need would therefore not be disenfranchised.

For understandable reasons, the investing community has always been opposed to the idea of non-voting shares. It reduces its power. More respectably, it argues that it makes companies too cosy, but that is because the voting shares are often held by a small, self-interested coterie. In the new language of polity the votes would be held by those with most to lose by bad performance - the workers and the major investors.

The stock market has always been largely a secondary market. This secondary market will continue as it always has, but it will not have a direct impact on the community, although the signals it gives out will contain important warnings or encouragement for the directors. It will be what it has always been, a casino. But, at long last, a casino without the power to affect the lives of the dice or the cards it is betting on.

CAPITALISM FOR THE INDIVIDUAL

Organisations will continue to be one of the major communities of society, although they may well be radically different in shape and structure. They must begin to take that responsibility seriously and to think of themselves as communities, for their own sake and for the sake of all who work for them. Because the better businesses are already heading this way, there is little doubt that community-thinking will lead to improved results as well as to a more decent capitalism.

In the not-so-distant past, the trade unions gathered more power unto themselves than was good for them or for the health of the communities where their members worked. Now it is the turn of the financial community to see its powers reduced. It will turn out to be for the good of all. It needs no laws to make it start happening; just the creation of two types of stock and the enfranchisement of the real assets of any business these days - the people who work in it.

PHILOSOPHICAL CONTRIBUTION IN MODERN TIMES

In reading through these chapters, the reader will find that through the centuries, philosophy as a subject contributed more than any other subject in the shaping of our lives, how we exist, how we behave and how we control our destiny. It is true though to say that on occasions, philosophy together with the sciences (with all the technological discoveries, the theories of evolution and genetics, the space explorations) and the arts, have contributed to our defiance of nature.

Psychologist tried to explain the bad and the good experiences and how they shape the individual. Some therapists maintain that it is the bad points, rather than the glorious moments that are most influential in personality development - in building the behavioural characteristics.

The author prefers the explanation of the idealistic philosophers. Where *anthropos* to them is *kalos - man is good.* It is this good nature of man that constructed the states, the democracies, with all the liberties to explore the sciences and to think. Thus moving forward in a positive manner.

'Story telling' through the electronic modes can only assist in preparing for the next twenty-five years of this millennium. Computing and systems influenced our lives, only to speed and send further out the public stories of history, politics and philosophy. Information technology has and will have a bigger role to play in the training and education of the non-privileged and all the races. Giving mankind new chances.

Politicians, in their patriotic moods, will ensure that everybody and everything in the environment will improve. Politicians are human too, and they bear their own sets of behaviour. They are not always the egocentric individuals that the mass media try to interpret. They have families and they want their children and future generations to live in harmony.

Philosophy for human behaviour for the individual, groups, society and the state (and the rest of the cosmos) will be well established in the next generation or two. Problems will be understood and solutions will be easier to find. Modern philosophers will integrate the knowledge gained from technology, the sciences and the logic gained from the great thinkers.

Humanity has more than two and a half millennia of philosophy (as we know it from written books), which can be relied on - to take us safely into the future. Neuroses, uncertainties, lack of confidence... will always be part of human nature. Philosophy with its vast thesaurus of assimilated knowledge will always assist in the harmonisation of people and the smooth running of the state.

PHILOSOPHY THROUGH THE AGES

Historically, there are records of philosophical thoughts going back eight and a half thousand years. Recent excavations in Cyprus and parts of the middle east, show constructions of people living in a civilised manner; where the gathering of big communities held discussions on morality and acceptable (or prohibitive) modes of integration within their legal and accepted state boundaries. Recorded thoughts, literature, poetry, art, religious beliefs, mathematical theorems and astronomical observations exist, proving that through the ages and since the Phoenicians, there have been influences on how humanity ought to behave and values which contributed to the evolution of thinking and the building of states. Individual standards, social norms and group deities helped with the setting up of laws within which the citizens found freedom.

People live in groups and humans choose to live in states, simply for what they can get out of society. Those who choose to live in solitude become recluse in monasteries and nunneries, or become thinkers in isolation high up in mountains. The remaining who wish to explore their interaction with others, integrate within the moral and legal demands of a government.

EMPIRES AND THEIR IMPACT

The Hittites, Phoenicians, Assyrians, Egyptians, Greeks, Romans and the Israelites brought influence on how we live, think and behave, probably more that any other known races. In recent times, the biggest influence to occidental, oriental and African countries - also, the smaller and unknown nations - came from the powerful European empires of Britain, Spain, France, and Portugal. The influence on thinking, believing, morality, language and the legal systems of the ancient, classical and modern powers on other peoples were not passed on peacefully. The people of lesser wealth did not (willingly) identify themselves with the leaders of the powerful nations. Changes in their way of living were done by force, oppression, slavery and exploitation. In doing so (for their own benefit), some European powers left a legacy for religion and some form of philosophical thinking.

It is universally acknowledged that the biggest influence came from the Hellenic states. The rest of Europe gained the lights of civilisation from the Greeks. Subsequently and based on the classical Greek civilisation, the rest of the Europeans spread the Grecian thoughts, in a diluted or in an altered version of rationalism which suited their needs. It is an acceptable fact that the Greek race has established the foundations of a holistic scientific knowledge and education, more than any other nation.

This influence subsequently spread as far as India and the rest of the known world. Obviously, the Greeks did not conquer the world with altruistic feelings and helping hands. Greece and all the states within Hellas were always poor. To sit back and think, to invent and to debate democratically, and to let their philosophers explore their logic, it meant that they had to exploit the material possessions of other races, or putting it more mildly, whenever necessary they had to trade with other people, or sell their know-how.

The Greeks, like many other powers, used strategic talents and polemic methods to obtain what they wanted in order to support their financial requirements back home. You cannot build a successful state unless you are prosperous. So for centuries the Greeks did just that. Even during the Roman occupation - with the leadership of Constantine The Great, they built the Eastern Roman Empire - Byzantium and for a millennium they isolated themselves within their Orthodoxy.

Their false feeling of superiority, their arrogance and their political isolation did not help; what with the Christian schism and the total separation away from the Catholics, the damage done by the Crusaders and subsequent Arab/ Ottoman attacks, it made them kneel; the effect being their complete surrender and capitulation to the Turkish invaders. Thus, with the conquest of Constantinople, the glory that was Greece went down. With the Ottomans capturing Byzantium and the Greek islands, Greece has never recovered. It is ironic that Greece with all its philosophy and civilisation is in need of therapeutic philosophy, more that any other state in Europe. The other two poor nations of the European Union, namely the old empires of Spain and Portugal are on the way to economic and social improvement. With the loss of their identity, the modern Greeks are still struggling to find their lost cause.

RECENT DEVELOPMENTS

A similar route for conquering other peoples was followed by the British and other European-based Empires. The British literature scene, the poetry, academia as a whole and philosophy, together with their language have contributed to the rest of the world's thinking, more than any other modern state. Writers and poets such as Chaucer, Shakespeare, Milton, Dickens, Shaw, Wordsworth, Coleridge, Byron, Bacon... (Only a handful of authors are mentioned here), together with all the British Philosophers, their writings, thoughts and concepts have become household names around the world. In earlier chapters of this book philosophers such as Hume, Burke, Mills, Locke, Hobbes, Bentham and their concepts on Utilitarianism, Rationalism, Conservatism, Socialism and Morality are discussed.

The British have also influenced their colonies with the English language (which will continue to be universally influential for many years to come), their parliamentary democracy, the legal system and of course the popular English sports; most of the ex-colonies play cricket and the rest of the world football. The Spanish and their inquisition spread Catholicism whether the American natives wanted it or not. The remaining of the European empires, as a legacy, they left mainly their linguistic communication and various dialects.

Germany and Russia only managed to conquer other European countries. It must be mentioned that, although Russia neither did nor conquer any other nation beyond Eastern Europe, their political system has definitely made an impact on many third world countries. The Soviet brand of communism influenced many other populations - East, West and African people. Although Leninism has failed, there are a few nations who still follow their own form of socialism. The Teutonic race has given us Kant, Hegel, Marx, Rudolph Steiner and their modern engineering know-how. The German contribution to philosophy goes well beyond the two big European-wide wars. Such works on Philosophy can only be admired.

INTERNATIONAL SCENE

The United States of America with all their material wealth, they have not yet made an important enough impact to match the philosophy of their European ancestors - the idealistic philosophy. On the psychotherapeutic scene, they certainly contributed enormously. Having followed the psycho-analytical concepts for a generation or more, they expanded alternative methods of therapy and psychology in general, through Skinner on behaviourism, Carl Rogers on Eclecticism, on the modern form of Counselling and similar academic and practical applications.

But, regarding philosophy - one can certainly accept that the American concept of consumerism has gone where no other materialism has gone before. It all started with cinematography and then with the active 'coca-cola-lisation' of the rest of the world, together with the silicon influence on technology.

Politically, their intervention in the Latin American countries, Vietnam, Laos, Iraq, Afghanistan, the ex-Yugoslavian states and the Middle East in general has done little to improve the individual and the state, as is philosophically understood. Ironically, within the circles of political philosophy, it is accepted that the backing of

Kuwait and other Moslem nations happened because of the empty Texan oil wells and the strategic geographical positions of Asia Minor, and not for the benefit of the people residing inside the warring regions.

MODERN PHILOSOPHICAL IMPACT

Philosophically speaking, the U.S.A.'s impact on the rest of the world is minimal in comparison with what the European philosophers have established. The U.S.A has been very successful in spreading the 'philosophy' of consumerism and the capitalistic freedom of trading. In an egoistic way, this is where the U.S.A. has excelled. With their vast natural resources and their technological success, the Americans will, for another generation or so, continue to influence the international political conflicts.

The existing political scene, through the United Nations Organisation, is influenced by the U.S.A. (more so now, because of the collapse of the Soviet block). But, with the re-formation and unification of Europe, also the European economic recovery, the political influence of the European Union will show improvement to their international relationships - thus benefiting the smaller nations, the third world countries and the Eastern European countries.

Economically, the E.U. will co-operate even more with the oriental, African and Latin American nations.

There are many other negotiated initiatives that the U.S.A. has taken, such as the Israeli-Arab conflicts. As yet, there is no solid progress. Certainly the U.S.A. initiative to resolve the long lasting Cypriot political conflict has reached a stale-mate. In any case, as this book is primarily interested in the influences of philosophy on human behaviour, apart from the Hollywood and the remaining of the consumerism type of philosophy which comes from America, it still remains to be seen how influential the Americans can be on the philosophy theme.

It is an undisputed fact that the Europeans cultures have established a philosophy which can be compassionate and therapeutic to the states around the world and the people living within their own chosen governments. It still remains to be seen what other impact the Americans can have on the rest of the world, philosophically speaking.

END

INDEX OF CHAPTERS (IN ALPHABETICAL ORDER)

ANTIPHON 39
CALLICLES   41
CAPITALISM FOR THE INDIVIDUAL 86
CICERO AND SENECA   52
CONCEPTUAL COMPREHENSION   5
COUNSELLING, STOICISM AND CHRISTIAN ITY 49
DEFINING POLITICAL PHILOSOPHY   28
EMPIRES AND THEIR IMPACT   90
EMPIRICISM IN PHILOSOPHY 20
EPICUREANS AND STOICS   50
IMPLICATIONS OF EMPIRICISM   72
IMPLICATIONS OF RATIONALISM   74
INFLUENCE OF CHRISTIANITY   55
INTERNATIONAL SCENE   95
LINGUISTIC EXPRESSIONS   77
MODERN ORGANISATIONS AND PEOPLE 80
MODERN PHILOSOPHICAL IMPACT   96
PHILOSOPHICAL CONTRIBUTION IN MODERN TIMES   87
PHILOSOPHY IN ANCIENT GREECE 32
PHILOSOPHY THROUGH THE AGES 89
PROTAGORAS   36
PSYCHOLOGY AND COUNSELLING JUSTIFICATION   69
PURPOSE OF PHILOSOPHY FOR HUMAN BEHAVIOUR 14
RATIONALISM OF KANT AND HEGEL   26
REASON AND REVELATION   67
RECENT DEVELOPMENTS   93
RISE OF THE NATIONAL STATE   65
SOCIAL PRACICES AND THE NEW MILLENNIUM   76
SOPHISTS AS THERAPISTS   30
SOPHISTS, THE SOCIAL PHILOSOPHERS 35
ST THOMAS AQUINAS 58
STOCK MARKET AND THE PUBLIC 84
THEORIES OF MORALITY   47
THRASYMACHUS 42
WORK RELATED PHILOSOPHY   78

BIBLIOGRAPHY

(ALL TITLES LISTED BELOW ARE WRITTEN BY ANDREAS SOFRONIOU)

MORAL PHILOSOPHY, FROM HIPPOCRATES TO THE 21ST AEON, ISBN: 978-1-84753-463-7

THERAPEUTIC PHILOSOPHY FOR THE INDIVIDUAL AND THE STATE, ISBN: 978-1-4092-7586-2 & 0952795655

PHILOSOPHIC COUNSELLING FOR PEOPLE AND THEIR GOVERNMENTS, ISBN: 978-1-4092-7400-1&0952795663

MORAL PHILOSOPHY, THE ETHICAL APPROACH THROUGH THE AGES, ISBN: 978-1-4092-7703-3 & 0952725339

2011 POLITICS, ORGANISATIONS, PSYCHOANALYSIS, POETRY, ISBN: 978-1-4467-2741-6

PLATO'S EPISTEMOLOGY, ISBN: 978-1-4716-6584-4

ARISTOTLE'S AETIOLOGY, ISBN: 978-1-4716-7861-5

MARXISM, SOCIALISM & COMMUNISM, ISBN: 978-1-4716-8236-0

MACHIAVELLI'S POLITICS & RELEVANT PHILOSOPHICAL CONCEPTS, ISBN: 978-1-4716-8629-0

BRITISH PHILOSOPHERS, 16TH TO 18TH CENTURY, ISBN: 978-1-4717-1072-8

ROUSSEAU ON WILL AND MORALITY, ISBN: 978-1-4717-1070-4

HEGEL ON IDEALISM, KNOWLEDGE & REALITY, ISBN: 978-1-4717-0954-8

MEDICAL ETHICS THROUGH THE AGES, ISBN: 978-1-4092-7468-1

THE MISINTERPRETATION OF SIGMUND FREUD, ISBN: 978-1-4467-1659-5

JUNG'S PSYCHOTHERAPY: THE PSYCHOLOGICAL & MYTHOLOGICAL METHODS, ISBN: 978-1-4477-4740-6

FREUDIAN ANALYSIS & JUNGIAN SYNTHESIS, ISBN: 978-1-4477-5996-6 & 978-1-4477-6010-8

MORAL PHILOSOPHY, ISBN: 978-1-4478-5037-3

PSYCHOLOGY OF CHILD CULTURE, ISBN: 978-1-4092-7619-7

BOOKS PUBLICATIONS BY ANDREAS SOFRONIOU – OCTOBER, 2012.

FICTION & POETRY

1. WILD AND FREE, ISBN: 978-1-4452-0747-6
2. THE TOWERING MISFEASANCE, ISBN: 978-1-4241-3652-0
3. THROUGH PRICKLY SHRUBS, ISBN: 978-1-4092-7439-1
4. SPEEDBALL, ISBN: 978-1-4092-0521-0
5. EXULTATION, ISBN: 978-1-4092-7483-4
6. DANCES IN THE MOUNTAINS – THE BEAUTY AND BRUTALITY, ISBN: 978-1-4092-7674-6 & 095272538X
7. FREAKY LANDS, ISBN: 978-1-4092-7603-6 & 0952725398
8. LITTLE HUT BY THE SEA, ISBN: 978-1-4478-4066-4
9. THE SAME RIVER TWICE, ISBN: 978-1-4457-1576-6
10. THE CANE HILL EFFECT, ISBN: 978-1-4452-7636-6
11. WINDS OF CHANGE, ISBN: 978-1-4452-4036-7
12. A TOWN CALLED MORPHOU, ISBN: 978-1-4092-7611-1 & 0952795620
13. EXPERIENCE MY BEFRIENDED IDEAL, ISBN: 978-1-4092-7463-6 & 0952725304

PHILOSOPHY & EDUCATION

14. MORAL PHILOSOPHY, FROM SOCRATES YO THE 21ST AEON, ISBN: 978-1-4457-4618-0
15. MORAL PHILOSOPHY, FROM HIPPOCRATES TO THE 21ST AEON, ISBN: 978-1-84753-463-7
16. THERAPEUTIC PHILOSOPHY FOR THE INDIVIDUAL AND THE STATE, ISBN: 978-1-4092-7586-2 & 0952795655
17. PHILOSOPHIC COUNSELLING FOR PEOPLE AND THEIR GOVERNMENTS, ISBN: 978-1-4092-7400-1&0952795663
18. MORAL PHILOSOPHY, THE ETHICAL APPROACH THROUGH THE AGES, ISBN: 978-1-4092-7703-3 & 0952725339
19. 2011 POLITICS, ORGANISATIONS, PSYCHOANALYSIS, POETRY, ISBN: 978-1-4467-2741-6
20. PLATO'S EPISTEMOLOGY, ISBN: 978-1-4716-6584-4
21. ARISTOTLE'S AETIOLOGY, ISBN: 978-1-4716-7861-5
22. MARXISM, SOCIALISM & COMMUNISM, ISBN: 978-1-4716-8236-0
23. MACHIAVELLI'S POLITICS & RELEVANT PHILOSOPHICAL CONCEPTS, ISBN: 978-1-4716-8629-0
24. BRITISH PHILOSOPHERS, 16TH TO 18TH CENTURY, ISBN: 978-1-4717-1072-8
25. ROUSSEAU ON WILL AND MORALITY, ISBN: 978-1-4717-1070-4
26. HEGEL ON IDEALISM, KNOWLEDGE & REALITY, ISBN: 978-1-4717-0954-8

PSYCHOLOGY & MEDICINE

27. MEDICAL ETHICS THROUGH THE AGES, ISBN: 978-1-4092- 7468-1
28. MEDICAL ETHICS, FROM HIPPOCRATES TO THE 21ST CENTURY ISBN: 978-1-4457-1203-1 & 978-1-81753-463-7
29. THE MISINTERPRETATION OF SIGMUND FREUD, ISBN: 978-1-4467-1659-5
30. JUNG'S PSYCHOTHERAPY: THE PSYCHOLOGICAL & MYTHOLOGICAL METHODS, ISBN: 978-1-4477-4740-6
31. FREUDIAN ANALYSIS & JUNGIAN SYNTHESIS, ISBN: 978-1-4477-5996-6 & 978-1-4477-6010-8
32. MORAL PHILOSOPHY, ISBN: 978-1-4478-5037-3
33. PSYCHOLOGY FROM CONCEPTION TO SENILITY, ISBN: 978-1-4092-7218-2
34. PSYCHOLOGY OF CHILD CULTURE, ISBN: 978-1-4092-7619-7
35. JOYFUL PARENTING, ISBN: 0 9527956 1 2
36. THE GUIDE TO A JOYFUL PARENTING, ISBN: 0 952 7956 1 2 & 978-1-4457-1448-6
37 PHILOSOPHY FOR HUMAN BEHAVIOUR, ISBN: 978-1-291-12707-2

INFORMATION TECHNOLOGY & MANAGEMENT

37. I.T. RISK MANAGEMENT, ISBN: 978-1-4467-5653-9
38. SYSTEMS ENGINEERING, ISBN: 978-1-4477-7553-9
39. BUSINESS INFORMATION SYSTEMS, CONCEPTS AND EXAMPLES, ISBN: 978-1-4092-7338-7 & 0952795639
40. A GUIDE TO INFORMATION TECHNOLOGY, ISBN: 978-1-4092-7608-1 & 0952795647
41. CHANGE MANAGEMENT, ISBN: 978-1-4457-6114-5
42. CHANGE MANAGEMENT IN I.T., ISBN: 978-1-4092-7712-5 & 0952725355
43. CHANGE MANAGEMENT IN SYSTEMS, ISBN: 978-1-4457-1099-0
44. FRONT-END DESIGN AND DEVELOPMENT FOR SYSTEMS APPLICATIONS ISBN: 978-1-4092-7588-6 & 0952725347
45. I.T RISK MANAGEMENT ISBN: 978-1-4092-7488-9 & 0952725320
46. THE SIMPLIFIED PROCEDURES FOR I.T. PROJECTS DEVELOPMENT, ISBN: 978-1-4092-7562-6 & 0952725312
47. THE SIGMA METHODOLOGY FOR RISK MANAGEMENT IN SYSTEMS DEVELOPMENT, ISBN: 978-1-4092-7690-6
48. TRADING ON THE INTERNET IN THE YEAR 2000 AND BEYOND, ISBN: 978-1-4092- 7577 & 0952795671
49. STRUCTURED SYSTEMS METHODOLOGY ISBN: 978-1-4477-6610-0
50. SYSTEMS MANAGEMENT, ISBN: 978-1-4710-4907-1, 978-1-4710-4891-3, 978-1-4710-4903-3
51. INFORMATION TECHNOLOGY LOGICAL ANALYSIS, ISBN: 978-1-4717-1688-1
52. I.T. RISKS LOGICAL ANALYSIS, ISBN: 978-1-4717-1957-8
53. I.T. CHANGES LOGICAL ANALYSIS, ISBN: 978-1-4717-2288-2
54. LOGICAL ANALYSIS OF SYSTEMS, RISKS , CHANGES, ISBN: 978-1-4717-2294-3
55. MANAGE THAT I.T. PROJECT, ISBN: 978-1-4717-5304-6
56. COMPUTING, A PRÉCIS ON SYSTEMS, SOFTWARE AND HARDWARE, ISBN: 978-1-2910-5102-5
57. MANAGEMENT OF I.T. CHANGES, RISKS, WORKSHOPS, EPISTEMOLOGY, ISBN: 978-1-84753-147-6
58. THE MANAGEMENT OF COMMERCIAL COMPUTING, ISBN: 978-1-4092-7550-3 & 0952795604
59. PROGRAMME MANAGEMENT WORKSHOP, ISBN: 978-1-4092-7583-1& 0952725371
60. THE PHILOSOPHICAL CONCEPTS OF MANAGEMENT THROUGH THE AGES, ISBN: 978-1-4092- 7554-1 & 0952725363
61. THE MANAGEMENT OF PROJECTS, SYSTEMS, INTERNET, AND RISKS, ISBN: 978-1-4092- 7464-3 & 0952795698
62. HOW TO CONSTRUCT YOUR RESUMÊ, ISBN: 978-1-4092-7383-7

www.ingramcontent.com/pod-product-compliance
Lightning Source LLC
Chambersburg PA
CBHW062041280526
45748CB00003B/1061